FUQ Racism

F.U.Q.- Full of Unanswered Questions

ISBN: 978-1-7357952-4-9

Printed by Power Of Purpose Publishing
www.PopPublishing.com
Atlanta, Ga. 30326

| CONTENTS

WHAT IS RACISM?

To understand racism, one must truly define it. Racism can be defined quite simply, but the implications that its definition has are much more complex. In easy words, racism can be understood as the act of treating another person or group of people differently based solely on the color of their skin.

It can include many other layers as well, such as discriminating against someone because they speak a different language, come from a different culture, and have a different religion than yours.

Racism only flows in one direction. It is the act of an individual, or group of people belonging to the majority of the population, behaving negatively towards those that are from the minority. In recent times, there has been the emergence of blatant racism exhibited by white people, who make up the majority of citizens in the U.S. against the Black people who make up the minority of the population.

Racism is a display of power. It takes power away from one group and gives unequal power to another. This means that the group that suffers at the hands of racism faces restrictions and limitations to their rights as human beings. They face limitations to basic human rights, such as the right to pursue any career they want, the right to occupy public spaces, and the right to feel safe and secure in the community they live in.

People who are subjected to racism are subjected to harassment and violence, which can be both physical and verbal. They're subjected to discrimination, biases, and stereotypes that take away from their right to individuality and expression.

It is also important to explore why racism came to be a concept in the first place. As it has been mentioned before, racism is a form of an unequal distribution of power. An unequal power dynamic can only have one purpose: to subject the one with the least power in their hands to circumstances that are essentially unfair and unjust because they have no other option other than to accept the situations they are in.

An example of racism was when Black people were brought as slaves to the U.S., to work, day and night on the fields that belonged to their white owners. These slaves were not allowed to leave and pursue a life of their own and were the victims of extreme discrimination, violence, and hate that they had no way of escaping from. They were barred from the basic human rights that the white people who constituted the majority had. They could not go to school, enter restaurants, shops, or even public spaces that were for white people only.

Although racism doesn't exist in quite the same way now as it did back then, it has only changed forms. While Black people were previously forbidden to enter public spaces that were designated "white" spaces, now, they have to live in constant fear of being attacked, tormented, verbally, or physically abused as they exist in those spaces.

They're still subjected to discrimination, such as not being selected for certain jobs, being stereotyped as criminals, drug addicts, and violent people, and having to work much harder to achieve the same level of qualifications as the white people in their community because of the inherent biases present in the system.

It's important to note that racism can never work in favor of the oppressed and marginalized. It is designed to concentrate power to one group. A Black person can never be racist towards a white person living in the U.S. because white people make up the majority of the population and hold all the power of the society.

Racism is not only about the explicit actions against a minority group. There are many underlying beliefs that fuel these actions. These beliefs have been passed on from generation to generation, for centuries, in a way that many people do not even realize the racist patterns underlying their actions. That is why combatting racism and purging these beliefs requires a conscious effort on the part of the dominant groups that make up a society.

ACTIONABLE ITEM

So how can we better understand racism? The first step to being more capable of identifying racism and noticing it in your actions, as well as in the actions of those around you is to accept that there is much to be learned. There are numerous websites, resources, books, podcasts, and shows that you can read, listen to, or watch in order to be more informed about the inherent racism that is present in society.

Learning about racism isn't just about following the latest posts on social media and sharing or retweeting them on your profile. While actions do matter, there is a level of change that needs to be done on a personal level before you go out into the world and perform certain actions on a public level.

Reading books by Black people about their experience, the impact of racism in their lives, and the ways in which they need non-Black, Indigenous, and People of Color (BIPOC) to change is crucial. Listening to podcasts by Black people who speak about the ways we engage in racism and how we can change is an essential part of the transformative process.

When we focus on what we're doing within our personal lives, such as the thoughts we have, the way we speak about racism in private, and/or the things we tell our children, it creates the foundation that is needed in order to combat racism on a grander scale. Until people learn how to catch themselves discriminating against someone based on skin color, culture, or religion, there can be no change to society.

Until we stop, reflect, and think about the ways we understand racism and how we convey these ideas to our family and friends, we cannot make a difference to how racism is carried out in the public sphere.

Being careful about the authors and the sources we use to learn about racism plays a role in the way we understand the concept. More often than not, people who do not fully understand racism and have never experienced it themselves write and talk about it in ways that end up being more harmful than productive.

Not only is it important to read about racism, it is also important to learn what anti-racism is. It is not enough to understand racism as a practice of injustice and discrimination. You must also thoroughly understand what it means to be anti-racist.

Anti-racism is when we identify and eliminate the racism in our society by targeting different structures of society, both public and private, changing policies, and reinventing our attitudes and practices. It is also about changing the power structures that currently exist, which place more power in the hands of non-BIPOC solely on the basis of race. When we are actively anti-racist, we are distributing the power that was previously concentrated in the hands of the few, in order to create a more inclusive and safe community.

There are many reasons why identifying and coming to terms with racism can be difficult for non-racialized or white people. While racism is extremely detrimental for those who are racialized, it provides numerous benefits for those who are not on the receiving end. Realizing that many of the privileges we enjoy in society are the result of racial discrimination against the marginalized is a bitter truth to face. When we are anti-racist, we go through the process of calling ourselves out on the benefits of racism that we have been thriving off of.

Being anti-racist is the next step once we understand what racism is. Coming to terms with white privilege and the ways in which non-racialized people are engaging, whether knowingly or knowingly, in the structures that enable racism, is extremely important. When we are anti-racist, we learn about how racism has been a part of the system for centuries, and that it is not always necessarily explicit. There are many implicit, underlying racist practices, beliefs, attitudes, and policies that are influenced by racism. We cannot identify and counter these unless we research the lived experiences of racialized people throughout history. This provides a clear perspective on how being non-racialized is a privilege that every non-BIPOC enjoys, whether they noticed it or not.

Being anti-racist means that we understand the necessity of diversity, inclusivity, and open-mindedness. Whenever we witness ourselves or others taking part in behavior that discriminates, places prejudice on, or stereotypes a certain group of people, we must make an active effort to fight against this behavior, recalibrate our mindset, and make a mental note of how our inherent beliefs have trained us to act in certain ways. Knowing that the beliefs regarding race that we have grown up hearing and learning about are not true, and that we are responsible for our own understanding of this expansive concept is how we lay the foundation to becoming anti-racist.

There are numerous people in society that neither add to nor counter racism. They believe that if they are not actively attacking someone based on race, they do not contribute to the problem. However, this could not be further from the truth. Based on the fact that modern society stands on a foundation made from a history of racism, everyone that does not belong to a marginalized group is part of the problem. It is not up to the oppressed to educate people and protest against the unfair treatment they receive and have been receiving for generations.

Even though marginalized groups all over the world still take out the time to protest against their oppression and teach privileged people about the racist history of society, it is not their obligation to provide us this service. It is up to the people who have thrived off of racism to make these efforts on their own. It is the duty of anyone attempting to be anti-racist to put in the time and energy to learn about racism.

Once we know what racism is, the only viable option is to move forward with this information and apply it in our lives, which is why being anti-racist is the only response to learning about racism.

Becoming an ally takes work, commitment, and the painful acceptance that you have been benefiting from other people's misery and oppression, whether you played an active role in it or not. There is always room for change, but being able to accept that a change is necessary is a crucial step.

TWO

HOW ARE RACISTS CREATED?

Racists are the result of a society that thrives and is built off of racism. People that are racists are the very people that need racism in order for them to live a life of privilege, opportunity, and power by taking away from the basic human right of others. In order to be racist, you must be insecure and unsure of your own inherent worth and capabilities to excel at life. When people are insecure and feel incompetent when it comes to excelling at life, they resort to the only other way to feel good about themselves: by putting other people below them.

However, the making of a racist is not this simple. There are generations of stories, beliefs, and behavior patterns that racists have been born into, which pushes them to become racists as adults and provides them with the confidence to justify their actions.

More often than not, you will notice that racists group together. This is because their beliefs are extremely problematic, hurtful, and lack the humanity and kindness that most people look for in the people that they interact with. When racists stick together, they can support each other's problematic beliefs and continue to create and raise a community of people who carry on their beliefs for generations.

The key factor behind the making of a racist is community. People who grow up in a community of anti-racists, inclusive people who do not discriminate and look down on people based on their gender, race, culture, and religion, are not likely to become racists. Children who grow up with racist parents, grandparents, siblings, and extended family will spend the majority of their adolescent lives, believing that what they have observed is the correct way to view others.

These children then have to make conscious, deliberate efforts in undoing what they have spent years learning, practicing, and understanding as "correct."

So how did racists come into being in the first place? They are the result of a political construction, known as racism. Racism was made to create class divides among people and is not based on any truth or scientific facts. Racism was created for a purpose and the people who enable, propagate, encourage, practice, and defend racism are the racists.

It is important to note that not everyone who benefits from racism is a racist. Many people do not realize the underlying injustice around them which helps them get ahead in society unless someone educates them or they educate themselves. However, when we continue to defend racist structures, standby and witness racism in action, or remain silent when an act of racism occurs around us, we are racist. To be silent in the face of injustice is not the opposite of being racist. The opposite of being racist is to be actively anti-racist.

When one group of people wants to dominate another group, for example, white people dominating over Black people, they need to be able to legitimize and justify their actions. One reason why Racists are created is because they need to adapt to a certain mindset in order to absolve themselves of the wrong that they are carrying out.

This means that when a group of people wanted to make Black people work as slaves on their farms and restrict all their access to basic human rights, they needed certain policies to support their actions. This was how they quieted their conscience and taught their children to practice the same behavior when they grow older. They needed these beliefs to justify their mistreatment and abuse of the Black people that they were using in order to become richer and more powerful.

When someone needs a set of explicit and implicit racist beliefs to flourish in society for their own benefit, they become racist. This means that to be a racist, you have to have an underlying agenda of staying in power. When you feel that your own capabilities are not enough to lead you to the positions you aspire to have, you perpetuate racist ideologies and practices that limit the number of people that can stand against you or challenge you—hence, paving your way to the top.

Racists are not created overnight. In order to understand the history behind the making of racist mindsets, we have to delve deep into history. There are numerous religious, political, cultural, medical, philosophical, and scientific ideas that date far back into history and are responsible for the collective racist way of thinking that we see today.

Religiously, people believed that Black people did not have souls, or were not human. This was used to justify the maltreatment that Black slaves were subjected to; it was believed that they did not possess the same level of humanness as their masters thus deserved any form of pain received from their masters. When many Black slaves began converting to Christianity after living in America for years, the lines that separated them from their Christian masters began to blur. It became confusing to determine whether they were still "soulless" if they practiced the same religion.

When religious justifications began losing their hold, people turned to science. Several scientific theories came about, which were used to explain how Black and Indigenous people aren't the same kind of humans as white people.

Why were these justifications necessary? As discussed previously, slavery was a widespread practice in America. The only way that white farmer rose in political and financial power was because they employed numerous Black slaves, and their entire families, to work on their farms without pay and for endless hours. They employed their children, the husbands, the wives, and anyone who tried to escape was brutally punished.

The slave trade formed a huge economy and benefited many white families who sold and bought slaves and did business with landowners. In order to encourage these landowners to invest in slaves of their own, they needed them to thoroughly believe there was nothing wrong with trading human beings and binding them to lifelong slavery.

Scientifically, studies were published, which claimed that Black people were diseased, subhuman, and inherently incapable of excelling anywhere else in life if it were not for slavery. People were told that their Black slaves did not have the mental capacity to be anything more than workers on a farm, hence they were doing them a favor by keeping them on their land.

They were also taught that Black people were an inferior race that was prone to disease and would eventually die out. This justified the killing of people in Africa because they were a "savage" race, which was nearing extinction. Hence, killing them was just speeding up the process of the law of nature.

This kind of mindset, although it seems difficult to believe now, was the key to many of the occurrences we see in history. The colonization of vast parts of the world by white travelers is the result of the inherent belief that white people are superior. The European travelers that roamed the world capturing and enslaving people, taking away their lands, and even killing them believed that they were entitled to do so – as these Black and Indigenous people were bound to die out anyway.

Of course, none of these scientific studies had any legitimate proof that made them believable. However, without them, the white conquerors of the world would not have found the justification to carry out their conquests. They truly believed that they were saving the world from a race that was not meant to carry on into the future, hence they continued with their genocide and enslavement for generations.

When we learn about the consistent racism present in society for hundreds of years, it is not surprising that so many people end up being racist. There are aspects of racism that are so deeply instilled in societal structures that it takes an immense amount of uncovering to come to the truth. This is why it is so important to not only pinpoint the racist tendencies within us, but to go through the process of eliminating this behavior from our lives.

ACTIONABLE ITEM

This leads to the question: how do we stop creating more racists in society? In order to stop bringing more racists into the world, we have to remember that nobody is born racist. They are born into racist communities, have racist parents, and/or are taught racist beliefs that they go on to internalize until they are made to reflect on their actions and ideologies. We can stop this by creating an environment of anti-racism.

To reduce the chances of someone becoming a racist, we have to keep a careful eye on the kind of exposure that children have. This does not completely eliminate the possibility of someone growing up to become a racist as an adult, but it has a significant impact on the probability.

When children are taught about inclusivity in schools, educated about the racist history of many societal structures, and taught about the many brutal and inhuman treatments that racialized people went through in order for the world to exist as it does, they will learn to be more aware of the society around them.

Because racists are created from the constant observation that people of color are inferior, do not deserve the same treatment as other people, are dangerous, or are not equal members of society – the role of preventing racists lies in the hands of caretakers. These are not limited to parents alone; teachers, counsellors, political leaders, and celebrities are all responsible and have roles to play in destroying the racist structures that uphold the society.

More often than not, we can't know what goes on within a household in terms of teaching children about inclusivity. That is why other members of a community can ensure that even if a child comes from a racist household, they are exposed to alternative ways of thinking through their school education, their peers, and the content they watch and read.

Until we can create a society that does not encourage or rely on racism to grow, we cannot guarantee that more racists will not be created. As long as people see the advantages of looking down on and discriminating against other people on the basis of religious, cultural, and racial differences, they will turn into racists or raise racists of their own. When there are no longer any divisions in society based on race, there will be no inclination for someone to use race as a means to marginalize another group.

Racists rely on the support of their community to thrive. They always have each other's support in carrying out acts of racism. This is why it takes a collective effort to put an end to racism. The fewer the communities that promote and encourage racism, the fewer the chances of racists emerging from these households.

THREE

WHAT IS RAGE?

In psychology, rage is a form of anger along with irritation and frustration. It is an intense emotion that we feel in the moment and could be triggered by someone questioning our integrity, making us feel unworthy or doubt ourselves. For example, if someone challenges our ego or we feel incapable or manipulating a situation to our benefit, we could feel a moment of intense rage.

As an emotion, rage is normal because it falls under the category of anger, which is a natural human emotion. However, when rage becomes violent and comes out in the form of physical and verbal aggression—there is a problem.

The reason why so many people need anger management classes and workshops that help them control their rage is that they have repressed their emotions for an extended period of time. When you do not allow yourself to feel healthy emotions as they present themselves, you let them build up inside you. When we don't express our emotions, the slightest incident can lead to a fit of rage that results in violent and aggressive acts that hurt those around us more than they hurt us.

Rage is an extremely personal emotion. We know this because when someone experiences a burst of rage, the reasons that cause it relates to them directly. When someone feels that their personal perception of themselves is being threatened, they can build up anger until it boils over into rage and manifests itself in a physical form.

Different people have different perceptions, beliefs, values, and ideas that are extremely personal to them. When someone or something challenges these perceptions, it can lead to feelings of aggression, hostility, and reactionary behavior as a form of defensiveness and protection.

An example of an outburst of rage could be if someone's deeply held religious or political views are challenged and they feel a sharp contrast between what they think and what they are picking up from the environment around them. The disconnect leads to a feeling of extreme anger or rage in an attempt to manage the conflict they are facing. If someone is made to feel as though their religious beliefs are not acceptable, they can lash out with rage to manage the threat they are feeling.

It is essentially a form of manipulation for the person experiencing rage to try and illicit the outcome that they want. It is also a form of immaturity—when you are unable to step back and observe a situation for what it is rather than for how it is making you feel about yourself. People who are able to pause and reflect on their feelings of anger without hurting anyone are mature and have higher emotional intelligence than people who resort to rage in order to "resolve" a situation and protect their nervous system from the incoming threat.

People who experience uncontrollable rage often find themselves displaying inappropriate behavior, such as assault, harassment, or even murder.

How does rage tie into racism? People who experience rage end up committing an act or acts of violence when confronted with people that challenge their beliefs. If someone feels as though a person from a marginalized group has access to privileges which they do not believe they have the right to, they feel rage. If a racist is in an argument with a Black person who is defending and standing up for themselves, they might feel the anger and rage rising inside of them.

This is because they have been made to believe that marginalized and oppressed groups should behave a certain way, be docile, and allow others to dominate them. When they come across a Black person who does not fit this image, their internal conflict rises. If someone has been letting this build-up for long, they will act out violently and aggressively and commit an act of racism.

Everyone feels anger. It is part of human psychology to feel angry when you are hurt or upset. The only time when anger and rage should be cast in a negative light is when the person feeling them hurts other people in the process. When they are unable to draw the line between what they feel and how they can express it, they can end up committing the gravest crimes.

As mentioned above, this happens when people are emotionally immature. People who belong to oppressed groups feel anger and resentment much more than those belonging to dominant groups. Marginalized people have faced injustice, harassment, and assault for generations—which has led to an immense amount of collective anger. However, they do not act out of rage and hurt other people because of what they are experiencing.

It is interesting to note that when we observe people protesting against racism, there is a huge amount of rage that fuels their actions. However, because they come from a place of emotional maturity and understand the implications of their actions, they don't act out of rage and hurt people; they protest on the streets and channel the anger they feel towards making a collective and systemic change after years of being oppressed.

This leads to another aspect of rage. When everyone feels rage, why do only certain people feel entitled to act from a place of rage, and hurt those around them? What gives some people the freedom to use violence and aggression to have their needs be met and their points of view accepted, while others cannot do the same? Why do racists have the freedom to attack people from marginalized groups, or anyone that threatens their beliefs and perceptions?

The answer is privilege. Privilege is the power that some people have over other people, which allows them to act, without consequence, in any way they want. Racists are privileged. They know that they can behave anti-socially without having to face the repercussions of what they do.

This allows them to use the rage they feel to take issues into their own hands and manipulation situations that feel uncomfortable to them. Privilege allows racists to survive in society with stunted emotional maturity and act unreasonably. It differentiates them from those who do not have the privilege to act without considering the consequences of what they do.

Why do people with privilege feel and exhibit more rage? Knowing that you have a certain privilege in society, be it with job opportunities, the respect your receive, or the way that you are always given the benefit of the doubt in any situation is a perk. As a non-racialized person who has the upper hand in society, everything works to your advantage, whether you explicitly notice it or not.

When the realization sets in that your position in society is not because of your individual achievements and character, but rather a result of privilege, many privileged people are riddled with anxiety. For example, men who see too many women applying for the same jobs as them are filled with rage – not because they genuinely believe that women are underqualified—but because they are afraid they will no longer have the advantage when it comes to securing any job they want.

Knowing that the privilege you enjoy is the reason you live a comfortable, secure, and safe lifestyle can cause anxiety. This is because people with privilege realize that everything that they have could leave them the moment they lose their privilege. When men realize that women could take away their privilege over jobs, they are filled with rage, resentment, and fear. They feel anxious about having to give up the luxuries they enjoy.

Rage against people of color works much the same way. When a majority of citizens with privilege realize that BIPOC in their community are capable of the same jobs, respect, and education as them, they worry about maintaining the upper hand that they have always had. Much of the politics we see around us thrives off of this anxiety. By telling the elite class that there could come a time when they have to share their luxuries with the people of color in the country, politicians profit off of their anxiety.

But what happens when people try to control this anxiety and take it into their own hands? What happens when a privileged white person sees a Black person with the same lifestyle as them? Or if they feel threatened that the people of color in their community could earn the same education as them and compete with them for the same jobs? They feel intense rage. They feel personally attacked and threatened because their entire belief system is challenged. Their belief that they are the rightful recipients of this privilege and that the marginalized people in their society are obligated to remain oppressed is shattered.

This is why people who are already oppressed never exhibit their anger. People who are oppressed do not have the privilege of feeling rage because they do not live a lifestyle that they are afraid of losing. They do not live a life of benefits and luxuries that were served to them on a silver platter—hence they are not anxious about change.

When faced with the possibility of change, the ones who could lose their unjust privilege are the ones that fear change the most. The ones that know that their lives will be uprooted and that they will have to make an effort to prove their worth feel terrified because deep down, they are insecure about not being enough on their own. They know that a hardworking person of color could come into the running for the same position that they got through their privilege, and they feel anxious and uneasy about having to face their feelings of inadequacy.

And because this unsettles the very foundation of current society, everyone who has ever benefited from their race and knows that they do not deserve the privilege that they have—feels rage. They feel rage whenever they see a marginalized person striving for success. They feel rage whenever they see protests, such as the Black Lives Matter movement. They feel rage whenever a person of color stands up to them—because they are forced to think about the fragility of their privilege.

ACTIONABLE ITEM

How can we counter rage? By holding the people in power and with all the privilege accountable for their actions. When they know that they cannot attack someone for wanting a better life for themselves and for defending their beliefs, they will be forced to control their actions. Once non-racialized people realize that the only way forward for us as a society is to take away their privilege and promote equal opportunities for all, they will have to quell their anger.

When politicians and lawmakers support diversity and inclusion and shut down dated ideas of dividing society by race, culture, and religion, the people who look to them for support and justification will have nowhere to turn to.

FOUR

WHY DO WE USE THE N-WORD?

The N-word is a derogatory slur used to insult and harm the people it is addressed towards. It is offensive and you cannot use it if you aren't Black. Several years ago, it wasn't as common knowledge as it is now – but the N-word has always been a slur that white people are not supposed to use.

What happens when someone uses this word to address a Black person? It leads back to a history of abuse, trauma, enslavement, and neglect. It was used to refer to Black people from the time of slavery and it always had a negative connotation. It made Black people appear less-than. It placed them below their white masters, as if they were subhuman.

It has now widely been accepted as an anti-Black word that is interlinked with racism. However, Black people can use this word whenever they want. This is because they have reclaimed the slur and with that, they have taken away the power that the word had. When a white person refers to a Black person as the N-word, it causes intense offense. When Black people use it to refer to each other, it lessens the power it has to offend them when used by someone who is trying to cause them harm.

There's a certain beauty in reclaiming a word. Whenever an oppressed group begin using the word that was originally used against them, they reclaim the power that the word had. They reduce its effect on them by making it common and normal in their community. Although it doesn't erase the history of abuse and racism that was associated with the slur, it prevents racists from having that same power over them that they used to.

The harm associated with the word isn't necessarily tied to the word itself. It has more to do with the history behind it. When people call Black people the N-word, it has a direct impact on their mental and emotional wellbeing. It is because it ties back to a lifetime of racism. When people are referred to by the N-word by those that oppressed them, they are forced to recall the financial, emotional, and societal turmoil that they have had to suffer for generations.

An interesting point to note is that the effect that the N-word has is unlike any other word. There is no slur that you can use against a white person or anyone from a majority group that is in power and has the most say in society. There are no terms you can use to refer to a white person that are linked to a history of oppression and force them to think about the lifetime of harm that both they and their ancestors have had to face.

This is why people use the N-word. When people call Black people the N-word, they know that they exhibit a certain level of power over them. They know that there are no words in response that a Black person could use to make a white person feel the same level of hurt and trauma.

Although white communities do have certain slurs that are used against them, they do not link back to a history of oppression. They do not tie back to trauma and they are only offensive to those white people who are guilty of taking advantage of marginalized groups. For example, if a white person referred to by a term that connoted being violent or oppressive, they would only take offense to it if they personally felt that they are violent and oppressive. However, when referring to someone with the N-word, there is no doubt that you intend to hurt them and that they will be offended.

So why do white people continue to feel entitled to using this anti-Black word? Why do they feel that they have the right to protest in favor of using this just because they did not mean to personally offend anyone? Many white people offer up the excuse that they were just copying a rapper or that they have always used it around their Black friends, who do not seem to mind. However, as part of an anti-racist movement, the shifts we make have to happen on a small scale before they happen on a large scale.

Even if a few white people make the effort of educating their friends on the negative connotations behind the N-word, it can start a chain of changes throughout their community. Black people are not obligated to explain the reasons why they find the term offensive – it has been explained time and again throughout history. As a white person, it is important to understand that by discontinuing the use of the N-word, you are letting Black people take back the power the word held over them. It is the first of many small steps that need to be taken for an actively anti-racist society, even if you cannot see the results.

By debating whether Black people can use the term or not, you are again creating an environment of dominance and control – which is the opposite of what anti-racism is trying to achieve. By giving the word back to the community it was used to harass, you let Black people decide on their own what they want to do with it. If they choose to use it to talk amongst themselves, it is not the right of any non-racialized person to dictate what is or isn't correct in their community.

Some people argue that even if it is not acceptable to use a word, there is no need to label it as the N-word. For example, when referring to the word as the word itself, and not directed at someone, it should to acceptable to say the word. However, labeling it as the N-word was originally done out of respect. To prevent anyone from using it, whether they were verbally harassing someone or just referring to the term in history books, it has now been euphemized as what we know today, the N-word.

Is it because society has become increasingly intolerant of expression? Or is it because we are becoming more aware of the cruel history of the word, and thus deciding to retire the word altogether unless it is being used by Black people? Many people have started to see the N-word as a taboo, because of the way it is currently discussed. If anyone hears someone use it within a professional setting, they could lose their job or be publicly shamed.

While it may seem 'too much' of a fuss over a word, words are never just words. They bring with them a history of insinuations. They can make or break a relationship. They can cause a lifetime of trauma for someone. And what's worse – many times, we do not realize the impact of the words we use. So, when Black people are openly objecting against the use of the N-word by anyone other than them, there is a reason. As anti-racists, it is important to listen to and follow-through with the changes that the marginalized groups around you are demanding.

ACTIONABLE ITEM

How can we get people to stop using this slur? A Black person voicing their objection to its use should be enough – but there are generations of stories that lead to why the word needs to be discontinued. It was used to minimize a Black slave into another aspect of a white person's property. It made Black people at that time see themselves as the less-than humans that white people made them out to be. Back in the time of slavery, Black people called themselves the N-word and accepted it as the reason for why they could not have the same lifestyle as their white masters.

If you go through literature from that time, you will notice that many slaves had internalized the concept of being the N-word that they were referred to by their masters. They used it to accept the treatment that they received, such as abuse – and made to live extremely degrading lifestyles. They would think that being given the slightest of "good" treatments, such as being allowed to sleep near their master's bed, was a sign of privilege for someone who was the N-word.

Hence, even many Black people have opted out of using that word in their families and in their social circles. Although they use it as a term of endearment reserved only for those that are the closest to them, they understand that its history is sad and upsetting. For this reason, they feel pain and anger at the treatment their ancestors felt, and out of respect for them have discontinued its use. That is not to say that they cannot use it. The word still belongs to the Black community—to do with it as they please.

What are some other reasons that Black people have chosen to reclaim the word? In the time of slavery, when white people referred to Black people as the N-word, they also created an internalized sense of dislike towards their own race. When Black people referred to each other as the N-word back then, they, too, meant it in a derogatory way. When the Black community uses that word now, they say it out of love, and it elicits a sense of belonging. They are taking away the hate that underlies the word and replacing it with acceptance and love—another way of taking away its power.

When a white person uses the word today, they are bringing back the same connotations that the word had in the past. That is why you will hear of numerous incidents where a white person hurls the slur at a Black person when they are upset. They understand the root of the word. They understand the hurt and trauma it will bring back and cause for the victim.

How can we stop using the N-word? Using the N-word is just another form of racism that needs to be addressed. There are several underlying behaviors in society that you may not realize are part of racism—but once they have been brought to your awareness, it is imperative for you to take the necessary actions and work towards changing the behavior.

The most effective way of doing so is by researching the history of the word and understanding the context that it was used in. Learn about the intentions of the people that labelled Black slaves as the N-word. It will ultimately make you realize why you need to remove the word from your vocabulary as well.

FIVE

WHY DON'T WHITE PEOPLE TALK ABOUT RACISM (IS IT FEAR OR IGNORANCE, OR IS IT DISCOMFORTING?)

White people do not talk about racism because there is a mixture of many aspects that come into play when the topic is announced. It isn't only fear – there is a sense of ignorance as well. The idea that racism will bring out the atrocities and torture that white ancestors have carried out in the past is uncomfortable. Having to accept that the world around us is standing on the foundation of these atrocities is even worse.

Although the ones that need to be addressing racism the most are white people – they are the last ones to arrive at the party. This is because it is a process of intense reflection, denial, and then acceptance. It is difficult to reflect on your own, and the behavior of your friends and family that you love. Having to understand how these behaviors could have caused harm leads to denial, because many times, the underlying intention may not have been to cause harm. However, once you accept that there are realities and consequences outside of your own circle, it will become easier to talk about racism.

This is in no way an easy process – as while Black people have been very vocal about discussing their history with their children, white people are quite the opposite. Black people need to teach their children about the oppressive and unfair treatment of the world around them in order to keep their children safe, aware, and be able to defend themselves against maltreatment. White people know that their children are not going to be faced with racism regardless of whether they are in school, college, or even when they begin working.

If anything, white people are aware that racism will have a positive influence on their child's life because of the system racism prevalent in every sector. They know their children are likely to earn more, secure better jobs, and have more power in society, even if there are Black people with the same level of skills and education.

It is challenging to talk about ideas and trends in society when they do not direct affect you. When there are injustices in the world that do not hurt the society, community, or social circle that you come from, it takes a certain level of humanity to bring yourself to care about the issue. When systemic racism in society does not affect the race in majority and the race that reaps all the benefits of that racism, there is a small chance that they will want to talk about it.

Not only is it difficult to talk about, but it is also even more challenging to make the decision to change certain behaviors and mindsets once the negativity has been identified. The process of identifying which behavior is a result of the racism around us means that we may have to make drastic changes in the lifestyles that have become the norm. It may mean having to accept that there are people whose lives may have been ruined by an act of racism that you or a loved one carried out. It would mean having to accept that it is you, and your community of white people, which oppressed the marginalized groups.

Being able to admit that you have caused harm also means you have to take the blame. Regardless of the context, no one is fond of taking the blame for anything. It means having to accept that you are, in fact, the bad guy. And for many people who believe they never caused any deliberate harm; this can be an impossible task to accomplish. In fact, even when people are clearly educated on which of their behaviors are harmful, they are resistant to accepting blame.

Another aspect of fear is the fear of having to face repercussions. The concept of 'white fragility' means that when you try to talk to a white person about racism, they feel extreme discomfort and become defensive. They are afraid that accepting that racism is a rampant issue in society would mean that they would have to pay the price for the damage that they have caused.

As discussed in an earlier chapter of the book, most white people are insecure about the position they hold in society. They have an underlying idea that they do not deserve the privileges that they live with. Having to accept that racism might have had a role to play in the privilege they now enjoy would be adding to their insecurities. It would mean having to accept that someone else could just as easily have taken up the position they have but could not—because of racism.

White fragility is a major problem when it comes to anti-racist discussion. This is because the ones dealing with racism on a daily basis do not need more education on how they can fight the system but the ones in power and the ones who have the privilege to work as allies and eliminate racism are unwilling to listen. These are the white people of the community. White fragility isn't only about ignorance and the refusal to confront the history you have created—it is about bringing anti-racist efforts to a standstill.

When all of a community cannot cooperate to fight racism, everyone else's efforts are in vain. Even if all the Black people in a community worked together to protest against racism and provide protection and comfort to the other people in their community, it would not bring an end to systemic racism. It would simply add to the emotional labor that BIPOC are already putting in in order to stand up for their community. The need of the hour is not for Black people to be made more aware of the injustices they face. The need of the hour is for white people to put aside their defenses and educate themselves about racism.

However, in most circumstances, when we need white people to listen and to work as active anti-racist allies, they do the opposite. Their white fragility causes them to withdraw, become silent, defend their actions, or even react with anger and backlash. Not only does this add to the oppression that people of color are already facing, it also acts as an encouragement to racists.

The racists in a society are aware of the protection they have. They know that regardless of what they do, the white people in their society and even the authorities will not penalize them. When they know that their community refuses to engage in conversation about racism, it gives them a free ticket to behave without any repercussions.

Not everyone who displays white fragility is racist. People who get defensive or angry may just be displaying normal human emotions when confronted with a bitter truth. It is no easy task to accept the wrongs that your people did and feeling a range of emotions from denial to anger are natural. However, the real work comes in when white people make the effort to shift away from the defensiveness they feel and open up to the idea that they may be wrong.

Even if someone is not racist, staying silent or defending racist behavior is a form of support. White fragility may not be a racist act in and of itself, but it is not anti-racist either. To counter white fragility, white people have to be anti-racist. They have to be open to the idea that there are aspects of their history that were horrific and shameful and that they are living off of the oppression of people who may now be their friends or colleagues.

To be silent when confronted with racism is only slightly better than being racist yourself. Although you may justify your behavior because you are not actively racist— it is important to remember that as a white ally, there is more to anti-racism than that. It is important to remember that to counter white fragility and be open to learning is only a small step of the way. Once white people have overcome their inability to engage in discussion about racism, they have to start speaking up against it and correcting those in their friends and family. They have to change their behavior and notice patterns of system racism wherever they go.

This is probably one of the main reasons why white people do not talk about racism. Because once they start talking about it without having their defenses up, they will have to come to the inevitable conclusion that their lives can no longer continue the way they are. This could mean a complete revolution in one's lifestyle.

Most white people do not have the capacity to make such drastic changes in their lives for an issue that does more good than harm to them. They do not see the reason why these additional efforts need to be made when it does not affect their life in any way.

Hence, the reason why white people don't talk about racism is a combination of fear, insecurity, ignorance, and the need to be inactive and stay silent. Even when a white person tries to be anti-racist, they will have to cut off ties with many racist friends and family and may even face backlash and negativity from their own community. Rather than go through with this struggle, they decide that this is not a battle they have the energy to face.

It takes a great deal of responsibility and ownership to look at your own actions and make the decision to change. It takes an even larger amount of responsibility to initiate those changes in the society around you, even when you are just starting with your close friends and family.

There are several layers to the responsibility—and to work through these layers is difficult for someone who does not see the need to care about racism in the first place. The realization that the injustices in your society are your problem as much as they are a problem for the individuals they are targeting does not come easy. In order for a white person to shed their white fragility, they have to be quite emotionally mature and equipped for responsibility before the discussion even begins. Talking to someone who immediately put up barriers and refuses to engage is a futile task. It may even lead to the opposite result—a Black person ending up having to apologize or comfort the white person who they confronted.

ACTIONABLE ITEM

How do we counter white fragility? The first layer that needs to be shed is ignorance. White people need to come to the collective understanding that they cannot ignore the oppression that their fellow white people are engaging in and that is integrated into the system they live in. Once they realize that community only functions when everyone takes care of one another—they have conquered the first layer: ignorance.

The second step is to counter their defensives. While it is natural to want to defend your behavior when someone tells you it is hurtful, they need to look at the bigger picture. The bigger picture is that once they know what they need to change—they no longer have to hurt anyone with their behavior. Knowing that once they put their defenses down, they will grow as human beings is the only way to shed this layer.

The last layer is fear and discomfort. The fear is of the discomfort that they know will follow once they open their perspectives to racism. The only way to counter fear is to remind yourself that uncertainty and discomfort is part of the process of reimagining society. No one can tell you what lies on the other side, but the only way to find out is to let go of that fear – or rather, to move forward despite it.

SIX

WHEN WILL BLACK LIVES MATTER?

So, when will Black lives finally matter? Now that we know the general reasons behind white people's hesitation towards talking about racism, the only question that follows is the question of when. When will white people finally decide that they have to put their privilege to use and fight racism? When will people finally realize that talking about racism as a theoretical concept and training future generations of marginalized children to tread carefully in their own home country is just not enough?

The catch with systemic racism is that even if all the privileged, non-racialized people alive today changed their behavior, it would not be enough. Systemic racism is about more than just realizing that you are part of the problem. It is about more than just discovering and accepting the ways in which you perpetuate racism in your day-to-day activities.

Systemic racism is designed in such a way that no matter what people do on an individual level—racialized people will continue to suffer the consequences of racism on a systemic level. It is the very foundation on which current society is built, hence, the amount of unpacking and change required to combat racism is vast.

It requires an uprooting of society from its very core. The only way racism can cease to exist is when race ceases to be a way for people to discriminate and classify other people. This is easier said than done because if you look back into history—the concept of racism has been part of modern society from the very beginning.

When will Black lives matter? Black lives have always mattered. Black will always matter. The only problem is the people benefitting from the oppression of Black lives do not want to accept this truth. The Black community has the power, the motivation, the years of struggle to push them forward and fight for their rightful place in society – and that is why people are afraid to let Black lives matter. They know that the moment they accept that Black lives are an integral part of society, they will be giving birth to a new society; to a new way of existing that they do not know of. The fear of letting Black people recognize their worth is paired with the fear of allowing society to change. When society realizes that the concept of racism is rooted in evil and oppression and that it must come to an end on a systemic level, the world will no longer be the same.

Black lives have always mattered. They have always been a part of society without whom most of us would not be where we are today. However, to accept that Black lives matter would be to accept that everything we have learned until today is in dire need of unlearning. So when will Black lives matter? They will matter when the ones in power are able to put their histories and their egos aside and initiate the changes in the system.

Until Black lives matter, all lives cannot matter. To say that someone "does not see color" is not the solution. To claim that explicitly standing up for Black lives is an extension of the main problem – using race to classify people – is wrong. This is because the generations of trauma that Black people have gone through cannot be brushed under the rug in the name of a new society that "does not see color." Their struggles, their pain, the turmoil in which they spend their lives must be recognized, reflected upon, and used to change the system.

Many people believe that ending the concept of race itself is the solution to racism. However, upon further contemplation, you will realize that this does not make Black lives matter. Instead, it groups them with every other race and discredits the past that has had such a huge impact on their community. The end to racism is not when we start seeing all races as the same. The end to racism starts when Black lives start mattering to the ones that are capable of changing life as we know it.

The question is not when Black lives will matter, rather, it is about when Black lives will matter enough. When will Black lives matter enough that the system will change? When will Black lives matter enough that we re-evaluate the histories we are taught in school and colleges? When will Black lives matter enough for the ones in power to accept their troubled pasts and claim responsibility for the wrongs that were committed?

Is there any way of knowing when Black lives will matter? The only thing that is known for sure is that for Black lives to start mattering, we cannot continue to be governed by the rules and regulations that currently exist. The law and order and the state of the government is the very core from where racism grows—and these cannot and will not change any time soon.

However, this does not mean that there is no light at the end of the tunnel. Just because a future where Black lives matter seems distant and difficult to achieve does not mean that it is impossible. As mentioned above, Black lives already do matter. They matter to the Black community and to the ones who have found love, support, friendship, and care in those communities. They matter to the people who use their white privilege to become anti-racist allies. They matter to the children who did not grow up being taught that Black lives do not matter.

The only problem is, they do not matter to the ones that can do something about system racism. They do not matter to the ones that can use their power in the government, in politics, in the public arena, and in education to ignite change. These are the people to who Black lives absolutely must matter – but they don't.

How do we get Black lives to matter to the ones that can become the agents for real, systemic change? For that, we have to understand how racism plays into the system and why the people in power need it to stay that way. The system is complex and made of a multitude of variables. The major variable that feeds off of racism is white supremacy. If we bring an end to racism at the systemic level, it would mean the death of white supremacy. Until this issue is confronted in broad daylight, the move towards anti-racism cannot progress either.

What is white supremacy? White supremacy benefits from the belief and the propagation of the belief that white people are superior to any other race. It is the encouragement of the mindset that individual people may be racist, and that they need to be further educated in order to deal with their racist tendencies, but that there is no inherent problem in the system. This helps white supremacists remain in power and exploit the minorities guilt-free, because the people in the community believe that racism is perpetuated by specific racist people instead of realizing that it is a part of the structure of society itself.

Why is it necessary for white supremacy to propagate this belief? It helps them avoid responsibility for doing the necessary work in society, not having to call themselves out on their problematic behavior, and remain in power, all while appearing to be allies by telling people to read up on racism. When white supremacy shifts the responsibility of change to the general public and away from themselves, they can continue benefiting off of the system while making people carry the burden of change. Not only this, but by doing the bare minimum of using social media or a public event to denounce racism, they lead people to believe that they are anti-racists as well – even though they are not.

White supremacy thrives off of creating a public illusion that Black lives do matter to the ones in power – but it is the behavior of the community that is getting in the way of real change. Why do white supremacists need this image to stay? Why are so many people a part of the dialogue that racism lies in the hands of everyday white people in the community and that it is them who need to unlearn racist beliefs, educate themselves, and become allies of anti-racism?

As mentioned, time and again, the concept of racism and being racist is not black and white. It is not only about who is and who is not racist, or how racists are bad and everyone else is good. It is about an entire structure of society that has made racism so integral in our system that you cannot divide people into racists and non-racists. In some way or the other, anyone who lives in a society that flourished off of racism has contributed and does benefit from it, whether they can catch themselves in the act or not.

However, the way that we currently understand racism has reduced it to the 'good' and the 'bad.' Anyone who talks about anti-racism is good, while anyone who is a racist is bad, and that is where the discussion comes to a standstill. But this is far from the case. Contrary to what white supremacy has made us believe, people do not become inherently good just by speaking up about anti-racism, and they do not become inherently bad if they are racist. This simply pushes away responsibility from anyone who thinks that as long as they don't call anyone the N-word, they are free from doing anything more for anti-racism. It places the entirety of the responsibility of racism on the people who openly abuse BIPOC communities – and these people aren't willing to accept their behavior anyway, as we have discussed before.

ACTIONABLE ITEM

This brings us back to the original question; when will Black lives matter? Black lives being of importance was never the issue; they have always been important – just not enough. The day when we openly dissect the system of white supremacy and the oppression it thrives off of will be the day when Black lives will finally matter enough. The day when we start discussions that question the structure of society that manipulates people of color will be the day when Black lives finally matter enough. The day when white supremacists are called out for their lack of effort and action and their surplus of meaningless speeches and empty promises, that will be when Black lives finally matter enough.

They must rise higher in importance than the way of living we see around us. It must become imperative to cater to the needs of Black lives and to give them the space and respect they deserve – regardless of the revolution it will initiate. The day when white supremacists are able to accept this reality and follow through with it with proactive measures that take away their privilege, that will be when Black lives matter enough to the ones that can give them the power they deserve.

SEVEN

WHAT IS EQUALITY?

Most people had a similar response when they first heard the phrase, 'Black lives matter.' Their response was that if we truly wanted equality, the phrase should be 'all lives matter.' However, this is far from what equality is when it comes to race.

By discrediting the need to give special importance to Black lives, we are actually taking away from equality rather than adding to it. By saying that the solution to racism is to emphasize how important each race is, we are not taking into account the underlying prejudices and systems in society that are unequal. Telling people that they should shout slogans of all lives mattering rather than give the spotlight to Black lives lets systemic racism off the hook, yet again.

How can all lives matter when we refuse to acknowledge the pain and suffering that one particular race went through and continues to go through on a daily basis? By insisting that all lives matter, and that this is how we achieve equality, we are denying the fact that there is more than just a surface layer of work that needs to be done.

The fact of the matter is that Black people legally have the same rights as white people. They are allowed the same rights in society when it comes to jobs, education, or social practices. The textbook equality that we read about already exists, but there is more to it than just these rights. By talking about Black lives in particular and by investigating the ways in which this equality does not exist outside of textbooks is how we achieve real equality.

Racial equality is about people having access to the same rights, liberties, and privileges as anyone else, regardless of race. It is about the removal of race as a factor with which to group, discriminate, or place judgements on people. Black people have the same rights to vote now as white people. They are allowed to express their opinions, own homes, and walk around in public spaces the same way as white people. However, there is no equality.

This is because the underlying system, the white supremacy, and the structure of the government still places more importance on white people. Even if Black people are allowed to vote, they rarely have any politicians and candidates who represent their views, stand up for them, and resonate with their beliefs. While they legally have a right to vote, there is no equality in the representatives that they can vote for. The problem with equality lies here.

There was a time in history when textbook equality itself was a vision of the future for Black people. Before they had the right to vote or sit in public spaces alongside white people and before they could go to school or express their opinions the same way as everyone else. However, while we have moved past these inequalities in society, we did not address the underlying beliefs that brought them into existence in the first place.

Having rights and being able to express those rights are two different concepts. You may think that Black people have the same opportunities for jobs as white people, but the underlying discrimination and the biases of corporations does not allow them to exercise this right. They can apply for the job, but if their employer has underlying beliefs about intellectual differences between Black and white people, they will not offer the job to a white person.

Additionally, if a workplace has never had Black employees, they may simply be too immune to the discrimination in their company. They may not even see the inequality behind their discrimination—because it lies deep within their belief system.

This begs the question, is proclaiming a place as non-racist enough to promote equality? Is declaring that BIPOC communities have the same opportunities the same as actually giving them the chance to pursue those opportunities? The answer is no. There is much more work in bringing about equality than making superficial changes to laws.

An example of this is media representation. Legally, all Black people are allowed to audition for roles and be in movies the way white people are. There are several shows and movies that have Black actors. However, how many of these Black actors are the lead character? How many of these Black actors are representing the true and authentic Black culture and not following a stereotypical storyline that white people believe to be true?

There are several TV shows where Black actors are used as 'tokens' to make a show seem inclusive. They have no character development or storyline of their own and their sole purpose is to be a supporting best friend or partner to the main actor who is white. Other times, they will have a stereotypical role, such as a child from a troubled home who lacks the love and attention of two happily married parents. This perpetuates the same beliefs –that Black people are incapable of cultivating loving homes, that their wives and mothers are extremely strict, and that the men in their families usually do not have a significant role in their children's lives.

Even though these Black actors have an equal opportunity to pursue a career in acting, they rarely get to be at the center of the stage. They do not get the same chances for representation, the diversity of roles, or the chance to explore the range of development their character could have. They are forced to fit into the mold of the 'typical Black character' that the media has created and maintained for years.

This is an example of how there is equality in the media industry – but not at the deep, systemic level that it needs to be at. The inherent beliefs about Black people still determines how they are portrayed in the media – while white people are free to take up a diverse range of characters.

What is the underlying inequality that needs to change? Performing basic actions of inclusivity actually contribute more to the problem than they do to solve it. This gives people the impression that if they ignore the root causes of inequality and bring a few Black people on set – they are now free of racism in their structure. It shows the hesitation in the media industry to look deeper into their practices and understand why they do not let Black people have any real representation or substantial roles.

The real work regarding equality is to make the necessary changes to the system that brought about inequality in the first place. Many times, workplaces, brands, and even celebrities take performative anti-racist steps such as having Black models, hiring a few Black people, or posting an anti-racist post on social media. However, their reluctance to break down the causes of inequality and make real changes is an indication that they just did this to avoid backlash from the public – not because they truly believe in equality.

An act of equality when it comes to workplaces would mean to notice the composition of employees in the company. If there are only two Black employees out of hundreds of white employees, a company needs to realize they cannot create products and services for Black people without having the necessary representation. They need to hire more Black people and reserve a specific number of employment spaces for BIPOC community members, knowing that they have not had the same exposure and experiences that white people had because of racism in universities, internships, and other workplaces. This would be an act of equality.

Similarly, if a white celebrity is asked to work in a film where there is little to no Black representation, or the Black character in the movie has no significant lines and follows a stereotypical plot, it is their obligation to either back out of the project or speak up about the dynamics of the cast. If they do not see any chances of their opinions being taken into account, they should leave the movie rather than stay on and act for a racist director and producer.

Equality is about more than just proclaiming that a space is open to people of all races. It is about understanding that white people will still have the upper hand and that institutions, people, and the system around us need to give certain leverage to Black people. If they cannot take the steps to do that, they are not promoting equality at a deep-rooted level. They're simply ensuring that no one can call them out for their injustices.

When we ask for equality, we ask for more than what white people already have. This is because Black people need more than white people to overcome the generations of injustice that they have endured. Telling Black people that they can apply for any job they want while simultaneously knowing that only a few of them managed to get into good universities is not equality. White people will still have more degrees, learning experiences, and corporate skills, which means that they will still get the jobs that Black people applied for.

An act of true equality would mean that companies hire Black people for the jobs they apply for and then offer them the additional education and skills they need in order to be as experienced as their white counterparts. True equality is about understanding that most Black people will not have the level of education as white people in your company because they were discriminated against when applying to universities. Hence, an act of equality would mean hiring them regardless of these differences and then doing the extra work of bringing them up to par with other white people.

Of course, most people see this as a grave injustice to society. The ones who believe that 'all lives matter, not just Black ones,' are the ones that cannot tolerate Black people being given more opportunities and leverages in society than white people. But if we are to bring true equality to society, we have to do more than just be non-racist.

ACTIONABLE ITEM

How do we promote equality? Being anti-racist means not actively being a racist and also not observing inherent racist behavior either. An anti-racist person or institution will take out the time to educate themselves on how to actively raise Black people up and give them the resources, jobs, and roles they need to really become an inclusive society.

You cannot be neutral if you want racial equality. You have to make a deliberate effort to go out of the way and bring Black people to the forefront. You have to let them get the representation they deserve. You have to actively seek out Black-owned businesses and do business with them. You have to give more scholarships to Black people and have more on board when launching a new product in your company.

It's important to note that this does not mean you are working towards reversing the roles where Black people eventually hold more power than white people. It is about removing the layers upon layers of discrimination that have held them down for years. And to do that, you have to place more emphasis on Black lives.

EIGHT

IS IT HARDER BEING BLACK?

If you take a look around you, it is obvious that being Black in a society fueled by white supremacy is extremely difficult. Not only do Black people not get the jobs they want, they are also paid lesser when they do. They are held back by tens of stereotypes, whether they are directed at their families, their personalities, or the way they talk or dress. They are also met with suspicion and hostility for simply going about their lives and existing as members of the society.

A white person walking down a street at night will feel terrified of being attacked by robbers or be scared of an angry dog barking from someone's yard. They know that they can call the police, identify the suspect and feel safe again. However, a Black person walking down the same street will feel terrified that a white person might see them, label them a criminal and call the police on them for absolutely no reason and without any proof. They might also be scared of an angry dog or a gang of thieves, but they know that they could never call the police for help. They will deal with their fear and their problems on their own – but going to the authorities for help is even more dangerous than letting yourself be robbed if you're Black.

This is a clear example of why being Black is much harder than being white; white people don't live with the constant fear of being killed from inside their own home, while Black people can never know when someone will accuse them of suspicious activity and call the police. One of the hardest parts about being Black is that they cannot turn to the authorities for help – which is the purpose of having a police force in the first place. When they need help, they try to resolve an issue on their own or within their community. They don't have an authority that they can turn to that will justly deal with their situation, while white people exploit their right to call 911 all the time.

A white person walking down the street may see an innocent Black person on the other side of the road, call the police and ruin that person's life forever. That Black person may even be killed on the spot, arrested without proof, or tortured and abused by the police. That Black person walking down the street has to live in constant fear of becoming the next target for an insecure white person – a fear that white people do not have to live with.

Whenever there's a nationwide emergency, such as the pandemic, mass unemployment, homelessness, and the like, the people who are most affected by it are primarily from BIPOC communities. Women of color are the most likely to be laid off when businesses start downsizing, and men of color spend weeks and even months looking for a job that pays enough to support their families – while white people not only get paid more, they're also less likely to suffer from the instability of the economy.

When Black communities face turmoil and law and order situations which require police intervention, they cannot turn to the authorities for help. This is why many Black youths are often stigmatized as being 'dangerous' or suspicious and find it harder to secure the same jobs as white youth.

The stigmatization of Black people becomes a self-fulfilling prophecy in its own way. Black people are treated poorly, looked at with suspicion when in a new neighborhood, terrified of the police in their own country, and dealing with the generational trauma of hundreds of years.

When these negative beliefs towards them push them further away from the rest of society and force them to take matters into their own hands to survive, they may get involved in crime or have higher cases of street fights. They also may have a higher chance of dropping out of school and starting to earn instead of pursuing further education because their families struggle to pay rent or send their younger siblings to school. When these issues are talked about in public platforms, people often forget to think about the context from where Black people are coming from and only look at what they can see – that they do not qualify for higher-earning jobs and come from broken homes.

This is more of a cycle of events that started from the day a child is born into a Black family: their parents struggle to care for them and do what they have to in order to tend to their children. If society gave them the same respect, and welcomed them into every realm of the society with open arms, they would not feel the need to distance themselves and build their own communities.

Black people who live in neighborhoods and communities that consist primarily of other Black people or BIPOC are more secure and feel safer because they are surrounded by like-minded people who understand their situation. If you reflect on the purpose of communities for marginalized people, you'll realize that they exist for protection and to create a society of their own for people who are not accepted and respected by the general public.

It's harder being Black because you only find safety when you're with people who have been through similar struggles as you. You have to rely on the community that raised you for support, love, and acceptance because the rest of the society frowns down at you and does not make you feel secure or safe. The fact that Black people prefer neighborhoods where they are in majority is proof that they find safety in numbers. The alternative to this is to live in a society where white people can call 911 on them for no apparent reason and have them locked away or harassed by police.

When people of color are in trouble, whether they are being assaulted by police in the middle of the street or whether they're being bullied at school for being darker-skinned, they usually fall back on each other for support. White people and any other non-racialized groups have isolated them from society to such an extent that they do not feel responsible for their wellbeing.

When people think about being responsible citizens – even when they're focusing on donating and volunteering to charities – the focus is on white people. When people see a Black person who has gone through immense hardship to build a better and more secure future for themselves and their children, they create doubts and suspicions in their minds about the legitimacy of that person's efforts. Whether you're a Black person who is scrambling to make ends meet or you're a Black person who has finally found financial security and educational prosperity, it's hard to feel as though you're a respected part of the very country you grew up in.

Being Black is hard also because you aren't given the same leverage as other people. If you follow the news and social media, you will see that white people are painted in a much more positive light – even when they've committed a horrible crime, as compared to Black people. For example, a white man who killed his children will be displayed in the media as a loving father who enjoyed long hikes and taking selfies with his children. The headline will read something like *'Distressed and Mentally Unstable Father of Two Makes Grave Mistake'*. The photos that accompany the post will show a smiling man posing with his kids while they take a family vacation. It's also more likely for him to get a lighter sentence on account of being mentally unwell rather than accept that he has committed cold-blooded murder.

On the contrary, anytime a Black person is shown in the news for something as minor as allegedly shoplifting, the image in the news will be of their mugshot, looking angry or upset. The headline will state something along the lines of *"Rebellious Teen with History of Theft Makes Another Attempt"*. People are less likely to look favorably at Black people or offer them any sympathies, and it isn't just on an individual level. With news outlets and media working day and night to make these subtle yet hurtful differences in the way they talk about Black people as opposed to white people adds to the fire.

It may seem like a harmless difference or even a coincidence that there is a discrepancy in media representation. However, that is far from the truth. Even if an individual journalist may not have explicitly thought of ways in which to make a Black person seem more criminal than a white person, there is a consistent pattern and a lifetime of history that has trained them to speak with such differing tones depending on race.

This means that should a Black person be pulled into a case – even if they are just a suspect who is later proven not-guilty, they'll live with the mark of this incident for the rest of their lives. Because white employers, professors, social circles, and the likes have become accustomed to always assuming the worst from any Black person they come across, they are more than ready to accept any negative records that they find. A white person, however, would be able to fit back into society and acquire a decent job even if they have recently served time in jail.

At every level of society, the way it is constructed makes it necessary for life to be harder if you are not white. The racism that lies beneath the surface in every part of the system, whether you think about the government, law and order, education, recreation, careers, and even rehabilitation centers, is designed to oppress Black people and cater to the needs of white people no matter how similar they are. The difference in their race is enough to put them on opposite ends of the spectrum.

Black people talk about the issues they face all the time. They are constantly trying to voice their opinions, express their distress, and seek help and support from members of society who they know have the power and capability to make a difference. However, their pleas, their anger, their resentment, and the backlash they face is all in vain. Vocal Black people are cast out of the society and made to look like criminals themselves. They face hatred, harassment, and become subject to further stereotypes, such as 'Black women are always angry.' Their feelings are dismissed instead of given the space to initiate change.

ACTIONABLE ITEM

How can we better understand the hardships that Black people face? Instead of labelling their protests as acts of 'anger' or dismissing them without paying heed to the message they are trying to convey, give their voice the space it deserves. Black people are tired of going over the same explanations time and again, but this doesn't mean that their conditions have changed. They have simply grown resentful of society because people refuse to listen, let alone make the necessary changes.

As an ally to anti-racism and someone who cares about the experiences of BIPOC, it is your job to notice the discrepancies around you. When you see news that is portrayed with a certain twist when it is about a Black person, convey your disappointment and hold people accountable. When you see BIPOC communities treated as though they are not as essential to the society as everyone else, do your part to get them recognition and help them with their struggles.

Go to Black-owned businesses, read books by Black authors, and attend the protests and lectures they organize. Encourage your white friends and family members to do the same and be an advocate. When you know that your voice can make a bigger difference, take advantage of your race. Use it to speak up for those whose voices are silenced.

NINE

WHY DON'T SCHOOLS EDUCATE ON RACISM?

As you may already know, racism starts when children are still young and impressionable. They learn it from their parents, their guardians, their neighbors, and their environment. When children grow up seeing their parents behave a certain way towards people of a different race, they internalize the concept and start behaving the same way. It's difficult for grown children to catch themselves exhibiting these racist patters, but it is not impossible. However, it would become much easier if children had a secure place where they could receive anti-racist knowledge when they are still young.

Schools should take up the responsibility of ensuring all children are educated about racism, what it is, how we engage in it on a daily basis, and the ways in which we can stop or speak up against it. Teachers make a lasting impression on children, and even if students go back home to a racist household, they will have access to an alternative way of thinking and are less likely to see racism as the only way of existing in relations to people of different races.

Schools usually do not educate children on racism. While they do occasionally encourage inclusivity and have workshops against bullying, there is not much depth to these lessons, and they are hardly applicable in real life. Children may have a vague idea that bullying is wrong, but if they exclude a Black child from their games in the playground, they will not realize that they are being unjust. This is because educating children on racism requires patience, perseverance, and an understanding of racism yourself.

The most important aspect of educating children on racism is the openness to accepting that there is evil present in society. This is the main reason why schools do not offer education on racism. If a school teaches children not to bully someone who comes to class in a wheelchair, they do not have to provide clarifications when a child points out that they have seen an adult bullying someone in a wheelchair at the park. They can simply tell them that anyone who bullies someone based on their abilities is a bully and needs to be reprimanded.

But when a child interrupts a session on racism and asks the teacher why their parents always tell them to steer clear of the Black family at the park, the teachers have no answer. To answer this would be to accept that racists exist all around us and are even raising the children who attend the anti-racist classes. The ambiguity surrounding how to address such concerns pushes the concept of anti-racist education far off into a distant future.

For starters, to approve this kind of education there would be a lengthy process where someone would present their stance and seek approval from the higher-ups. As mentioned, time and again, the implications of racism exist in every sector, which includes the educational sector as well. This means that this kind of education is unlikely to be approved. After all, it would be difficult for anyone in authority to encourage the teaching of a syllabus where a country's own history is displayed in a negative light.

To answer children's questions of why their parents engage in racist behavior, teachers would have to imply that a child's parents are wrong to do so This could result in backlash from parents, especially in a school which primarily has white students. Young children love going home to talk about their school day with their parents or guardians and there is no guarantee that these adults will not be outraged when they hear of anti-racist education.

Because any kind of change starts with changing the way we talk to our children and ending generations of toxicity, educating children on racism would mean the beginning of the end of racism for the future. This sounds similar to the dream of anyone who has been fighting against racism all their lives, but it is the nightmare of anyone that needs racism to thrive – which is almost anyone who is not part of the BIPOC community.

When the ones advocating for the inclusion of anti-racist education in the school system are in the minority, the chances of them succeeding with their appeal are low. The very foundation that schools are built on depends on propagating racist beliefs, even when it is now more subtle than before. Children must all grow up to believe certain facts about their government and the history of their country in order to remain loyal and patriotic.

Additionally, they need to be kept under the impression that there is goodness and kindness prevalent all around them – an idea that would be shattered if they learned about racism.

To teach children about racism would mean to understand it at some level. Educators are rarely equipped enough to grasp the concept on their own, let alone convey these ideas to anyone else. Instead of teaching children to be actively anti-racist and instilling in them a sense of acceptance for all people, they could instead create a sense of pity or disdain towards people of color. In an attempt to get students to understand that racism is wrong, they could use the explanation that 'you should be nice to Black people' rather than elaborating that discrimination based on race is wrong. Because education at this level plays a role in the core beliefs that children have as adults, it's important to have educators that understand the extent of responsibility that lies in their hands.

Not educating students about racism is more of a political issue than anything else. If young students discovered that their country was built on racism and that their grandparents were probably abusive and vile towards people of color, they will not remain docile and accepting of the rules of society. With the realization that the environment you live in is based on lies and harm, there comes an urge to disregard everything you have ever been taught and be disillusioned by society. Instead, schools choose to remain silent over these issues to maintain a sense of peace and blind acceptance.

ACTIONABLE ITEM

What can you do to combat the education sector's reluctance to educate on racism? There are now several different sources from where children acquire their vast reserves of knowledge. They watch videos on YouTube and religiously tune in to certain TV shows every day. They play with other children, read books, and now have access to social media as well. All these areas of interactions are areas where they can learn about anti-racism as well. You can encourage them to watch videos that promote inclusivity and read books that their school doesn't provide. They can read about history, art, and culture from sources that aren't tainted to present a certain worldview.

Make sure that your children are not exposed to influencers or bloggers who openly display racist tendencies, have a discriminatory air about BIPOC, or look down on anyone that does not conform to a whitewashed perception of beauty. There are many influencers now that promote body-positivity, as well as several pages that break down the reasons why only certain features are considered beautiful in society.

Children consume content at their own pace. If you do not monitor what they are watching, they will find content on their own. Rather than leaving them to navigate through a universe of information which may or may not be useful for them, designate their time in front of a screen to learning about concepts that will make them kind and responsible adults. If there are any pages or channels that subtly or directly shame people based on race and skin color, make sure you distance your child from them and inform other parents who might be unaware.

Of course, any parent who takes these measures is clearly doing their part towards being more anti-racist. But what about the children of parents who are not doing their part? Who will provide this education to children who do not have access to teachers or caregivers that are willing to put in the work? When neither educational institutions nor parents want to take the first step towards unlearning racist behavior and passing on their new mindset to children, who steps up to take that role instead?

One solution is for teachers to bring anti-racism conversations into day-to-day conversations with their students. Even if there isn't a proper class where they can dedicate a specific amount of time to anti-racism education, they can casually use moments throughout the day to talk to their students about what is being shown on the news, how the students are feeling, and what emotions are coming up when they hear about the violence taking place in their country. They can talk to them about their thoughts on BIPOC protests and what might have caused citizens to take to the streets to protest for their rights.

It's important to find ways around the obstacles present in the system if you are going to bring about any real change. Although it might be years before a designated anti-racism syllabus is included in every school, the educators who know that this is a discussion that needs to take place will find ways to incorporate it into their routine. It's essential for caregivers to have at least a vague idea of what their students' emotions are regarding what is happening in their country. This can help them console and comfort children who are distressed by the news and cannot find anyone to talk to, or to reeducate the children who do not understand what is going on.

Many children can only look towards the media representation of BIPOC and their guardians' explanations of current events – which may or may not be anti-racist. Having some insight into the kind of information these children are acquiring helps educators guide them towards a more anti-racist understanding.

Some ways that anti-racist educators can go about including this in their daily conversations is by further educating themselves about what anti-racism is, how to practice it, and what kind of activities constitute anti-racist work. The more equipped they are to handle a student's questions, the easier it will be for them to have these discussions. They can also bring in a few news clipping or recent events to bring up throughout the day and ask students what their thoughts are regarding those events. They can talk to the children about what kind of conversations they hear outside of school related to these events, and whether they reflect the points of view the students hold as well.

If possible, educators can bring in a few novels or books by Black authors, or show a few videos every once in a while by someone who has experienced racism, is an active anti-racist, or has an engaging and lighthearted way of conveying anti-racist information without overburdening or distressing a student. As long as an educator maintains some level of exposure to anti-racist discussion for their students, they will be playing a major role in changing students' perceptions of racism. As long as it remains a forum for conversation and understanding while staying within the limits of a casual discussion, most parents or even the heads of education cannot raise an issue with it. After all, discussing current events has always been a tradition within classrooms and does not need to have a syllabus that outlines how to go about the conversation.

Educators can also have these discussions amongst themselves and reach out to anti-racist allies who can further improve their grasp on the concept. They can look for resources on their own or ask their colleagues for suggestions. It's vital to check the source of the news an educator brings up in the classroom as well. Depending on the media outlet, the news could be misrepresented or conveyed in such a way that subtly changes your reaction towards it – as mentioned previously. If educators bring in voices that are authentic and align with the voices of BIPOC, it becomes easier to talk about it in class. Being careful of your sources is part and parcel of redesigning the understanding we currently have of racism and anti-racism, and it starts with careful consideration of the context and background of each news source.

TEN

WHY DON'T PARENTS EDUCATE KIDS ON RACISM?

For parents to feel the need to educate their children about racism, they have to have a level of compassion and empathy for what they see around them. Parents who do not see how racism could affect their children will also not see why their children need to learn more about the concept, either.

Children from the BIPOC community will always have an understanding of what racism is – how they will be discriminated against by their peers at school, and how they should interact with authority figures. Even if a Black child does not know the name of the discrimination and biasness they are facing, sooner or later, every racialized child will realize that they were the victims of racism – whether they knew it at that time or not.

However, in most situations, parents of Black children will try to keep their children as safe and as distant from racism as possible by sticking to schools where the majority of children belong to the BIPOC community. They will also teach their children to keep a distance from groups of white students and only to trust people who look like they do in order to protect them. The earlier on a child is instructed on who they can feel safe around and who to keep their guard up around, the less likely it is for them to become victims of racism that hurts their self-esteem and damages their sense of self.

Parents of white children do not offer their children this education simply because they do not need to. They do not need to tell their children to be careful around other white children or instruct them on how to speak to authorities because they know that their children's lives won't be endangered if they come into contact with police. Black parents fear for their children's lives because they could quite literally be killed in a police encounter while coming home from school or playing in the playground.

When there is no fear associated with racism towards your child, a parent will not feel inclined to educate their children about a concept that has nothing to do with them.

On the contrary, children from the BIPOC community are taught about the unavoidable racism they are bound to experience almost as soon as they are ready to start school. This begs the question, if Black children are obligated to learn about the ways in which they could be subjected to racism and discrimination, why are white children not equipped to learn about the ways in which they may be complicit in this racism or how they can prevent it if they see it taking place? Why are white children not taught to be inclusive, to be open towards all the other children they meet in school, and not to decide their company based on what someone looks like?

Racism thrives for one main reason, which is that if someone isn't actively being racist, they aren't actively being anti-racist either. Staying silent when they should be speaking up and fighting for change is the core ideology behind which racism continues to be passed on from generation to generation. Essentially, racism is supported in every facet of life, regardless of whether people are willing to see and admit it or not. When someone doesn't put in the effort of educating their white child about racism, they are supporting racism. When someone stays silent upon hearing that a Black child was bullied and sent to the nurse at school, they are supporting racism. It is an uncomfortable idea to accept, but it is the only way for people to be pushed into making the necessary changes.

Parents need to understand that by not talking about anti-racism with their children, they are supporting the racism that is bound to happen at their child's school. If they do not think that their child is old and mature enough to be able to deal with such information, they are supporting racism. When children from BIPOC communities can grasp the concept and have to face this discrimination from such an early age, why are their white peers not capable of putting in the minimal effort of adding to that racism?

The sooner children learn about the cruelty and injustice in the world, the quicker they lose their glowing, optimistic view of the lives they live. The sooner that children have to discover that there will be adults and children alike who want to cause them harm, the earlier they will be forced to mature and have their guard up. No parent wants their child to have to leave their innocence behind prematurely, but unfortunately, BIPOC children are forced to understand the realities of their society from very early on.

Learning that the community you come from is complicit in harming others and that there are children in your school who will be discriminated against on the basis of your skin has a similar effect on white children. Although they still maintain their childish, optimistic view of the world for many more years than Black children, white children whose parents teach them about racism from a young age are more mature than the ones whose parents do not educate them.

They learn to be more observant of their surroundings. They may point out instances of racism within the classroom or call out an adult who is discriminating against someone. For parents who come from a racist community, even if they are not actively racist themselves, these observant and vocal children could become a source of embarrassment and social fallouts among their friends and family.

For white parents, the cons of educating their children on anti-racism far outweigh the pros. The most that their children will gain from an anti-racist education is the ability to be compassionate and not judge people by their appearance, while the list of cons is endless. The children may get into trouble at school, they may not be able to enlist in certain programs or clubs, or they may tarnish a parent's reputation amongst a racist crowd. If white children start attending protests and rallies with their Black peers, parents will be terrified and worried about their child's wellbeing.

Overall, the reason why white parents do not feel inclined to include anti-racist education in their conversations with their children is that they want to protect them. They want to protect them from the realization that children their own age live much more difficult lives than they do merely because of their race. They want to protect them from becoming aware and critical of the flaws and cracks in the society they have always seen as their home as a safe place.

They want to protect them from the realization that they themselves, their friends, and any other white person they know are the culprits behind this injustice. Because the sooner a child comes to terms with these realities, the sooner they will start looking down on the same country, which they should be looking up to. And a change of this sort is unbearable and scary for a parent who has never experienced anything of this nature before—because their parents protected them the same way.

ACTIONABLE ITEM

Is there a way for parents to start educating their children about racism without overburdening them beyond their age and robbing them of their childhood innocence? For the same reasons that parents from BIPOC communities are compelled to teach their children about the reality of the world they are going out into, parents of white children should be compelled to educate their children about racism as well. When white people develop a sense of compassion and responsibility for the wrong that occurs in society – especially at a level where they are directly involved – they will realize how important it is to give their children an anti-racist talk. The only way that we can reduce the stress and turmoil that young Black children have to go through when they enter school is if we make sure their white counterparts are doing their duty to reduce this racism as much as possible.

Merely educating the oppressed on the oppression they are inevitably going to experience only normalizes racism further. Although it is necessary for racialized children to be made aware of what they should look out for, it's actually more important for non-racialized children to learn about how to be anti-racist. This is the only way that we can break the cycle and move towards an anti-racist society. Currently, with only Black people being the ones who understand the level of oppression they face, there is no radical change that is taking place. Children are learning, just like their older sibling and their parents in the past, how to tiptoe around situations and how to avoid getting into an argument with the police; they are learning to stay away from racists, but the racists are not learning how to stop and change their own behavior.

For that, we need parents who are willing to step out of their comfort zone and equip their children with this necessary knowledge. We need parents who are willing to unlearn what they were taught in school and reeducate themselves for the sake of BIPOC children who are being stereotyped and bullied in schools across the country. We need parents who are willing to look beyond their own household and understand the impact that their conversations with their children will have on other people and their children. Perhaps, a white child who learns about racism will be vocal and defend their Black peers in an incident of bullying or perhaps they will never encounter a situation where they make use of the knowledge they gained until they are much older. Regardless, the difference they would make to a Black child's life by simply deciding to be anti-racist is immense. This will have an effect on other students as well because children learn from observing each other. A white parent may not see how their anti-racist education could possibly be beneficial for their own child, but they must learn to see how it will bring peace to the life of another child.

Of course, simply having a conversation about anti-racism is not going to bring an end to racism in all schools and public places where children gather and interact with each other. It can only bring about a small change at an individual level. However, the real change that this would bring with it is that white children would realize they have a responsibility to fulfil and that the struggle against racism is not just for the BIPOC community to face alone.

Parents might find comfort in getting in touch with other parents or communities that help with anti-racist resources or have gatherings which educate children as a collective. Whatever means they decide to resort to, the main obstacle that they have to counter is the fear that they are exposing their children to the harshness of the world prematurely.

To counter this fear, they have to remind themselves that teaching children to be inclusive and anti-racist does not bring them any harm. Sooner or later, their children will learn about racism on their own terms, and if their parents had a neutral stance regarding the topic, they could sway their loyalties in either direction. Having a child who grows up to become an active racist who brings harm and pain to other people's lives is far worse than having a child who understood from early on that they have a duty to their community to be anti-racist.

You may also be helping another child with your efforts. Children who come from a racist family may not have access to the resources that you use to educate your child. If any other these children become friends with your child, they may learn that there is an alternative way of viewing the world apart from what they have always observed from their parents. It helps children from the BIPOC community point out allies and understand who they can trust when it comes to countering the racism they face.

ELEVEN

HOW CAN WE COMBAT RACISM?

If you feel that there is something inherently wrong with society and that you need to change the way things are— you're already ahead of many others. Being able to realize that the inequality and discrimination you see around you is a problem that needs to be addressed is the first step to working towards finding a solution.

Many people aren't able to see past their privilege and look at the world around them. They aren't able to identify which areas of their lives are a result of their privilege. They believe that what they have achieved is from years of hard work and struggle – while refusing to understand that there are entire sections of the population that work tirelessly with no results.

Once you have established that racism is a problem you are willing to fight against, you must remember that staying neutral is not a form of protest. Just because you are not explicitly engaging in racist behavior yourself does not mean that you are free from perpetuating racism. Combatting racism requires active, deliberate anti-racist work.

This means accepting the reality that your world will no longer be the same. You'll have to sit with the realization that being white has given you a privilege that other people do not have. You have to realize that as a non-racialized person, you have a life that is much easier and free of strife as compared to racialized people. Of course, everyone has challenges in their lives and problems that they wish they could resolve but being discriminated because of your race leads to a sense of powerlessness and hopelessness that non-racialized are privileged enough not to experience.

Combatting racism means looking at the world around you and noticing that it isn't as inclusive and progressive as you thought it was. It means that you have to read between the lines wherever you go. For example, you will have to start noticing when the news portrays certain people a certain way as opposed to the way they describe other people. You'll begin to start doubting what you see and hear, but it is all part of the unlearning process.

Unlearning what you know about race is vital in becoming anti-racist. If you stick to the same education and societal concepts of your past, you cannot move towards a progressive future. You will have to put in the work of finding newer, more eye-opening ways of thinking. You'll come to realize that there are discrepancies in everything around you, and racism lacing every aspect of society just waiting to be caught.

You can have to prepared to lose friends and family who do not agree with your changing perspectives. When people begin anti-racist work, they're often caught up in backlash and outrage from their friends and family who feel called out and attacked by their words. You'll have to be ready to speak up against your own family when they display racist behavior and differentiate yourself from them by being vocal about your views.

Working towards being anti-racist means having the end-goal that one day, society will not discriminate against people based on their race. It is having the goal that people will not have to live with fear and be oppressed simply because of their culture, religion, or the color of their skin. This means that whenever you catch yourself in the fact of forming biases or following pre-existing biases, you have to put in the effort of changing. Sometimes, you will only realize after someone points it out that you have exhibited an underlying racist belief, but as long as you are willing to hold yourself accountable and change, you are doing a significant amount of work.

Holding yourself accountable means acknowledging that there are things you will do and have done in the past that were born of out racism. It's important to have the openness to change your perspective and accept your shortcomings, because real and permanent change always starts from within you.

Being anti-racist means that you have to be a model of anti-racist behavior that you wish to inculcate in other people. There are certain aspects you have to teach other people and there will be debates where you educate other people about the problems in their behavior, but you cannot jump to this stage without observing yourself first.

Many people realize that in their fight for anti-racism, they will have to give up going to certain restaurants, following certain celebrities, and change their political stance. They will realize that their anti-racist tendencies could cost them their job or lead a falling out with their social circle. When they discover that becoming anti-racist has these repercussions, they often take a step back.

This is why you need to think about your own alignments, your lifestyle, your behavior before you make the decision to be anti-racist. You cannot be an anti-racist if you simply frown at people who are racist and then proceed with your day. You have to make the conscious decision to become a part of change.

ACTIONABLE ITEM

So, if you're looking for ways to combat racism, ask yourself, are you willing to change your lifestyle? Are you willing to speak up if your colleagues or your boss exhibit racist behavior? Are you willing to file a petition against an institution that has racist policies? Do you realize that you will have to let go of some of your favorite actors, or change who you vote for in the next election? Remember, being anti-racist is not about 'not seeing color,' it is about seeing color everywhere you go and recognizing the discrimination that happens because of it.

For example, if your family has always held a certain prejudice against Black-owned business, the solution is not to state that you purchase from business based on quality and that you do not 'see color.' The anti-racist solution to this is to seek out Black-owned businesses and purchase from them exclusively. It is about wondering why there are not enough books by Black authors on your bookshelf and purchasing them. It is about sitting down with your children and calling out the people in your lives that are racist and teaching your children that those people are racists.

Being anti-racist is not about avoiding race and acting like nothing you do is fueled by racism. Everyone that is not from a marginalized community has benefited from racism and is guilty of perpetrating it in some way. You cannot avoid the blame that there are things you did which were racist on some level. But on the bright side, you have to remember that the only way that change comes about is when you realize that you are responsible for it.

If you never saw the problems in your behavior, there would never come a time when you would decide to turn your behavior around.

TWELVE

WHAT ARE THE NEXT STEPS?

As part of your journey towards anti-racism, you must become an ally. Becoming an ally, as a non-racialized person is much different than being a 'white savior.' You are not above the people that you are allying with. You have been born into a certain segment of society which has placed more power and privilege in your hands, but that does not make you superior.

From what we discussed in Chapter 1, becoming an ally means understanding what racism is through the lens of those who actually experience it. It means revisiting what you know and unlearning it in order to make space for the voices of the BIPOC community. You can do this by attending protests, such as the Black Lives Matter protests that take place. You must also actively seek out information on your own. While it is true that Black people have a vast expanse of information to provide you, as part of the work that comes with being an ally—you have to put in the effort of educating yourself. Relying on the education that marginalized people give you only exhausts them further, so the advisable course of action is to learn from those who have already written books, made videos, and published articles about their experiences.

Once you're well-equipped with this knowledge, you need to use it to become a platform for the BIPOC community. This means that you lessen the burden of educating others that they have by amplifying the voices of those who have already spoken. For example, some people confuse being an ally as being someone who can speak *in place* of the marginalized community. This is not what it means to be an ally. Being an ally means raising the voices of the people you are allying with. It means distributing the information they have already given out to those who are asking to be educated. It means taking on the task of helping more people come within reach of Black voices and their experiences so that they, too, can become aware.

The next step is a branch of allyship. Once you have committed to being an ally, you need to make a deliberate effort to stop more racists from spreading their agenda. You have to keep a careful eye on the people in your community for signs of a bigoted mindset, or an indication that they may act out of racism and hurt someone. While we often discuss ways in which to react to a racist or how to deal with racist behavior, we rarely talk about where racists are coming from and how we can reduce the number of racists in society from increasing.

As discussed in Chapter 2, racists rely on the support of their community to keep them going. They cannot work in isolation if they know that they will be met with backlash for their actions. That is why it is imperative to call out the racists in your neighborhood, workplace, community center, etc. so that they know that they will not have your support when they're looking for backup.

It's also important for you to work towards educating the children and impressionable people in your community so that they are aware that the racists in the society do not represent the only kind of perspective you can have about race.

Accountability is a key element in countering this racist behavior. If you hold people accountable for their actions, they will know that they cannot act from a place of rage and anger and take the law into their own hands. When racists realize that they cannot verbally, physically, or emotionally assault someone because they are struck with a surge of rage and hatred, they will be forced to keep their emotions on a leash.

Currently, there are numerous incidences of racist white people lashing out at the Black people in their neighborhoods, either by pointing guns at them or screaming and verbally assaulting them. They have taken it upon themselves to convey their dislike of anyone of a different race than them on behalf of their whole neighborhood. It is your job to hold these people accountable for their actions. Chapter 3 states that people act out of rage when they know they won't have to face any consequences. If you speak up against this racist behavior around you, you'll encourage others to do the same. With a lack of support, racists have to quell their anger and control their behavior – to an extent.

One way of holding people accountable is by no longer allowing anyone you know to use the N-word without questioning them for their choice of language. Unless you're talking to a Black person who uses the word, you should not be tolerating your friends, family, colleagues, or anyone else to use the expression. As mentioned in Chapter 4, using the N-word is a form of racism, whether people are aware of it or not. Many people have only picked up the word from songs or the media and may not realize that using the word is inappropriate. However, if you allow it to continue, you're adding to the problem.

You can begin by educating people about the implications behind the word, but if they continue to use it, you need to call them out and reprimand them for their behavior. It's important to realize that if someone continues to use the word even after discovering the history it holds, they are engaging in racist behavior.

It's also important to conquer your fear and discomfort. As mentioned in Chapter 5, fear, ignorance, and discomfort are all reasons why non-racialized people avoid talking about racism. As long as you stay defensive, you can never overcome these feelings. You have to be willing to accept that there are going to be discussions and discoveries that will lead you to the realization that you've been a racist in the past. You may even realize that something you've unknowingly been doing your whole life is inherently racist. You cannot let this defensiveness stop you from learning about racism.

When people become defensive, their focus shifts towards proving themselves innocent rather than coming up with ways they can change. If you're having a discussion with someone who informs you that your organization has a racist hiring policy, your job is not to defend this policy or list out the contributions your organization has made to society. Your job is to learn about ways in which you can create a new policy and engage in discussions that help you understand the problem more effectively.

Nobody enjoys having someone call them an oppressor or inform them of the injustice in their actions. No one is a fan of being told that the lives they live are the result of their privilege and not entirely because of their hard work. Furthermore, no one wants to tell their children that they have made mistakes as parents and that they have not been the best of role models. But if you're going to hold other people accountable, you have to start with yourself. When people give you an opportunity to change your actions, look at it as a privilege to get the chance to be better rather than a personal attack.

You'll also have to peer deeper into the political stance you have. What are your preferences? What are the histories and ideologies of the politicians you support? Chapter 6 discusses how white supremacy thrives off of racism. Take a look at the people you give your vote to. Even if it's just one vote, you have to make a conscious decision about voting for people that align with anti-racist ideologies. In the end, the public, even as a collective, cannot make palpable changes if the government does not allow these changes to happen.

Because the BIPOC community has been living a life of discrimination and injustice, you cannot remain neutral if you wish to see a change. This means that you will have to go out of your way to accommodate people of color in areas where they have not had the privilege to be before. In your corporations and organizations, if you have certain criteria that you know fewer Black people will be able to meet, you have to revise the rules. In fact, as discussed in chapter 7, you have to place more importance on giving marginalized people the exposure they need. When looking through job applications or resumes, keep in mind that one reason why a Black person may not have the same experiences as the white applicant is because of the racism they faced in their past. Use this knowledge and your privilege to give them these experiences so you can end the cycle.

Part of using your privilege is about actively seeking out ways in which you can benefit BIPOC. This means looking for Black-owned businesses and restaurants and preferring them over others. It means learning about Black authors and purchasing their books. Be an avid observer of the aspects of your lifestyle that you can change to help people of color. Another example, as discussed in Chapter 8, is that you can send editorials to local newspapers when you see them portraying news about Black people with a negative undertone that they otherwise do not use for white people.

As always, change has to happen at all levels of society. This means you'll have to research the kind of books your child reads for class. You'll have to find out more about the education your children are receiving and whether there are any classes or lessons on anti-racism. Even if your local school does not impart this knowledge to your children, you can do so on your own terms. Many schools hesitate to have such classes, but if you can get other parents on board and push for more anti-racist education, the school might be willing to make some changes. Of course, this requires time and commitment if you want to convince other parents of the importance of this education.

As discussed in Chapters 9 and 10, children are often kept in the dark about what it means to be racist, how they can be anti-racist, and the history behind racism. This is because people are confused and hesitant about having these conversations with their children. They may be unsure of how to answer their questions, or afraid that children will find out that the society they live in is riddled with injustice and oppression. This is bound to happen, but as long as you're open to educating yourself, you can always find ways to answer your children's questions. As for taking away the shiny optimism about society from your children's perception, you have to keep one thing in mind: the children of BIPOC communities were never allowed to have this optimistic view of society. From a young age, they were taught how to stay safe and steer clear of the numerous people who would hurt them. If these children have to grow up before their time, your children can learn about how to be anti-racists from a young age as well.

CONCLUSION

We must act *now!* Countering racism and working towards recalibrating the society we live in is not a task you can put off until tomorrow. There are many doubts and skepticisms that may come into your mind; you may feel as though you are not prepared or knowledgeable enough to begin the work. However, no one is ever fully ready to embrace these kinds of changes in their lives.

There will never come a time when you will be fully prepared to take part in anti-racist work. There is a huge expanse of learning that you'll come across on the journey – from learning through the people you meet or finding flaws in your behavior when someone else points them out. No one is perfect from the very beginning of a process, but as long as they keep an open mind and are perceptive to the advice given to them by the people they trust, they are ready to begin the work.

Being afraid of change goes hand in hand with being afraid of growth. People who are willing to change and learn at any age and at every stage of life are the ones who are the most likely to grow as individuals. When you widen your perspective and come to accept that you are part of a problem that is bigger than yourself, feel humbled and ready to do what it takes to bring change.

When you realize that your individual efforts, no matter how minor they seem to you, are laying the foundation to change, you won't hesitate to keep discovering newer ways to make a difference.

When we, as individuals, use the privilege given to us to bring equality, we're breaking the cycle of racism that has existed for generations, and also work towards creating a more inclusive society.

CPSIA information can be obtained
at www.ICGtesting.com
Printed in the USA
LVHW010405190922
728691LV00023B/1041